Mediumship Made Simple

A Step by Step Guide to Connecting With Spirit

Lynn Lloyd, M.A.Ed.

Mediumship Made Simple
A Step by Step Guide to Connecting With Spirit

ISBN-13:
978-1460971925

ISBN-10:
1460971922

Printed in the United States of America

Design and layout by Lynn Lloyd

Foreword

"Here's a book you must read! Lynn Lloyd, a noted author and herself a medium, puts mediumship in a totally new perspective that probes the very essence of our existence as evolving souls. Her masterful treatment of this often misunderstood topic will change not only the way you look at mediumship but the way you look at yourself as well."

Joe H. Slate, Ph.D.

Licensed Psychologist and Professor Emeritus,

Athens State University

Dedication

This book is dedicated to my Guides for *ironically* believing in me and especially to my husband, whose encouragement and unwavering support have made all my dreams come true.

About the Author

Lynn Lloyd is a survival evidence medium, which means she is able to connect the plane of the living with the plane of the dead. When spirits communicate with her through feelings and emotions, she is able to convey messages to the living based on the thought energy she receives from them. She is a certified hypnotherapist and studied under Dr. Joanna Starr at the New England School of Hypnotherapy.

Contents

Introduction

Most books on mediumship development are written by mediums who were born with the ability to communicate with spirits.

As a medium, I have the utmost respect for super psychics such as John Edward, James Van Praagh and Sylvia Browne but most of these gifted people were aware of their ability from a very early age.

I was not one of these child prodigy mediums who were born aware of my gift. And yet I am a medium. I often pick up names, messages, the way someone looked, their mannerisms and even phrases of speech unique to them.

All my life, the idea of psychic phenomena and predictions interested me. I certainly believed others could do it—just not me. I bought book after book promising to develop my untapped psychic abilities. I practiced the exercises until my head ached. All the development strategies, it seemed, were dull mental tasks, involving intense meditation and imagery. Some of them even came with neatly packaged CDs. But not once did I ever have an insight, prediction or anything I could deem as intuition.

I felt most of the books out there attempted to pigeonhole mediumship and even mediums for that matter.

The truth is we all have the ability to communicate with spirits.

This communication takes desire, practice and a dedication to learn how to go beyond our five physical senses and open ourselves to the sixth-dimensional world that exists within us all.

Everyone's development is different. Everyone's energy is different. But everyone has the ability to develop some sort of mediumistic talent.

The ways one receives information from The Other Side varies widely but through practice and finding your mediumistic niche, I am certain you can develop the ability as well.

What Is Mediumship?

Mediumship is a term used to denote the ability of a person (a medium) to produce psychic phenomena of a mental or physical nature. The term is commonly used to describe a person who is able to facilitate communication with spirits of the deceased or other non-corporeal entities, either by allowing the spirit to use their body through trance or by using extrasensory perception to receive and relay messages from the spirits.

Although there has been a recent plethora of television shows based on mediumship, mediums have been around a long time.

Even the ancient Greeks employed the use of scrying—gazing into water—to communicate with the spirits of the dead.

In the Bible, First Samuel, Chapter 28: 3–25, there is an account of the Witch of Endor being consulted by the Hebrew King Saul. The witch was asked to speak to the recently deceased prophet Samuel to ask his advice about an upcoming battle. Samuel's ghost appeared and predicted King Saul's downfall. Saul died in battle the next day.

Joan of Arc, a peasant girl who lived in fifteenth-century France, claimed to have visions of the Virgin Mary. Crediting her divine guidance, Joan led the French army in many victories against the English who later captured her. She was tried by an ecclesiastical court and found guilty of heresy. Sentenced to death, she was burned at the stake at the age of nineteen. Years after her death, she was declared an innocent martyr and in the early twentieth century she was eventually canonized.

One of the world's most famous prophets was Nostradamus who lived in France in the sixteenth century. His collection of prophecies is still widely studied today. It is believed Nostradamus received messages by scrying, either with water or by flame-gazing.

In the late nineteenth century, mediumship made a comeback in Great Britain and the United States with the rise of Spiritualism as a religious movement.

Unfortunately many fraudulent people saw an opportunity to cash in on the grief of others and this hurt the rise of modern Spiritualism. Spiritualism, which began in the late nineteenth century, is a religion similar to the Christian faith. However, Spiritualists believe spirits of the dead return to communicate and pass messages and wisdom about the afterlife.

Even Abraham Lincoln employed the technique of table tipping during his presidency!

Two mediums who have made a significant impact on recent spiritual history are Edgar Cayce and Helena Petrovna Blavatsky, who was said to be able to produce flowers and other items out of thin air.

Some notable mediums of contemporary times include Jeane Dixon, Allison DuBois, John Edward, James Van Praagh, Sylvia Browne and Jane Roberts.

Types of Mediumistic Ability

Mental   Communication takes place between the spirits and the medium. The medium mentally *hears, sees and feels* messages from the spirit, which she may or may not relay to the sitter (person who is receiving a reading).

Trance   A medium allows a spirit to use her body to communicate. There are two types of trance mediumship. *Partial trance* mediums are consciously aware during the period of communication while *full trance* mediums allow their bodies (including speech and mannerisms) to be completely controlled by the spirit communicator.

Physical   The medium's body and energy is used by the spirit to manifest loud raps, levitation, items, such as flowers or jewelry, ectoplasm (a substance of spiritual energy — often visible in photographs) or manifestations of the spirit itself (a visible entity).

Groundwork for Meditation

In this book, you will explore a vast world that exists within you — the spirit world.

As you open to this world beyond the veil, you will learn much about yourself. You will uncover your beliefs and values. You will discover the innate ability you have to communicate with the Creator, your Guides and deceased friends and relatives.

This process will be a joyful spiritual awakening that promises to fulfill you in ways you never imagined possible.

The meditations in this book are not about coercing your active mind to go blank but rather about encouraging you to *focus* on concepts that will bring a sense of intuitive peace and spiritual understanding to you.

Meditation can be done practically anywhere but, if you choose, you can create a sacred space in your home or even in your office.

The addition of candles, religious objects or crystals is completely up to you. Use your sacred space only for meditation and keep the area clutter-free.

You can meditate in silence or perhaps you prefer soothing music as a background.

A sacred space is not required, however, you may find it easier to get in touch with your inner voice if you meditate in a place you've set aside solely for that purpose.

Remember that you will want to meditate when you are feeling fresh. The act of meditation opens you to other dimensions. Do not attempt to meditate when you are tired, sick or after imbibing alcohol.

Basic Meditation Exercise
(Finding Your Inner Sacred Space)

When you perform any of the meditations in this book, you will first want to do this basic meditation exercise to relax your mind, body and spirit, thus enabling you to tap into your intuition.

- If you've created a sacred space, sit quietly in it for a moment and take a few deep breaths.
- Close your eyes.
- Mentally release all aches and pains, all racing thoughts and feelings.
- Ask God (or your Deity of choice) to surround you with protective White Light. Visualize this Light around you. Here, nothing can harm or frighten you.
- Begin to focus on your breathing. Imagine you are inhaling the White Light into your body. Visualize it traveling to every fiber of your being.
- Exhale slowly, visualizing all your worries, aches and pains leaving your body with your breath.

- Relax every aspect of your body. Start with your toes and move up your body, relaxing every muscle, each limb. Pay special attention to those places where you carry your tension. Remember to relax your facial muscles, your jaw and the tiny muscles around your eyes. If you have trouble relaxing, first tighten the muscle and then relax it.

- Now envision a system of roots that connects you to the center of the earth. Imagine these roots sprouting from your feet and traveling through the ground straight to the core of the earth.

- Visualize a cord of White Light, which emanates from the top of your head and connects you to the Universe. Feel this connection. Know you are a part of everything that exists—God, the earth, other living beings, water, air. Affirm it by saying, "I am connected to all that is." Feel the emotions associated with this wonderful connection.

- In your mind, create an inner sacred space. It may be a lush park or a tranquil beach where you can listen to the rhythm of ocean waves. Sense your inner sacred space with all five senses. How does it look, smell, sound? Do you taste anything? How do you feel? Experience the emotions.

- Enjoy the peace of your sacred inner space.

- When you are ready to return to the physical world, thank God for all the things in your life for which you are grateful including discovering this peaceful place inside yourself.
- Open your eyes.
- Take a few moments to assimilate with the physical world by taking a bath, eating a healthy snack, taking a walk, anything that will ground you by engaging your physical senses.

Before the meditations that follow in this book, I will advise you to go to your *inner sacred space*. The more you practice this simple meditation, the easier it will be for you to quickly find your inner sacred space.

Before long, intent and a couple of deep breaths will carry you immediately within!

Spirits, Spirit Guides and Gatekeepers

If you are familiar with terms used by mediums, then you've no doubt heard the terms spirits, Spirit Guides and Gatekeepers. However, you may not be familiar with how they differ from each other.

A spirit is a soul—a being who has either incarnated on the earth plane (lived a life or lives on earth) or who has not.

A Spirit Guide is a soul with whom you have made a celestial contract to help you learn life lessons, guide you in making decisions that are in your best interest and help you develop spiritually.

If you've seen Sylvia Browne on *Montel*, then you've heard her talk about Francine. John Edward refers to his Guides as "the boys". I have a couple of Guides and I'm fortunate enough to know who my Spirit Guides were when they were alive but knowing who they were is very unusual and not necessary.

Everyone has a Guide or two, or maybe more. Sometimes, you will have the same Guide throughout your life and sometimes these Guides might change based on what challenges and issues you are facing in your life.

You knew these souls a long time before you decided to be born. They care about what happens to you and they care that you learn the lessons you set out to experience when your spirit decided to jump into a body. Think of Spirit Guides as a kind of celestial Dr. Phil.

However, your Guide is not here to do all the work for you. The Guide is simply here to facilitate learning for you based on what is in your best interest.

Ryan is one of my Spirit Guides but I always have free will. He does not control me in any way, shape, form or fashion and he never intrudes. I have to ask for his help and guidance.

Spirit Guides are rarely people you knew in this lifetime. Certainly, your loved ones in spirit can offer you advice and guidance but the comparison would be like going to a friend for life advice as opposed to someone with Dr. Phil's professional expertise and sense of detachment.

A Spirit Guide is always, always, always available to you.

A Guide is a spirit on whom you can call anytime, anyplace, anywhere.

Everyone also has a Spirit Guide who serves as a Gatekeeper.

Your Gatekeeper is a powerful spirit whose purpose is to protect you from negative energy and negative entities. Anytime you do not feel comfortable speaking with a spirit, you can call on your Gatekeeper Guide to surround you with White Light and shield your energy from negativity.

Never feel guilty about calling on your Guides or Gatekeepers. Although they are always there for you, other spirits are not so available. They, like living people, don't answer every time you decide to call. That's why it's a good idea not to *summon* spirits.

It's not necessary for you to know your Spirit Guide's name or who they were in life. Sylvia Browne's guide, Francine, told Sylvia her real name. Sylvia didn't think it fit so she promptly changed her guide's name to Francine. Francine doesn't mind. Spirit Guides don't care what you call them—just call them!

When my husband wanted to connect with his Spirit Guide, I told him to tell me the first name that came to mind for him. He said, "Karen."

"Okay, Karen it is," I told him. He balked. He couldn't conceive of a Spirit Guide with such a common name as Karen but his Guide seemed to like the name. Now he communicates with Karen on a daily basis.

Spirit Guides and angels are two different beings. According to some mediums, a Spirit Guide has usually, if not always, incarnated in a body at one time or another. In other words, they were once alive. They know what it's like to live in a body, therefore, they have the ability to sympathize with you.

Angels, as I am told by my Guides, have never incarnated in bodies and never will.

Getting to Know Your Guide Exercise

Would you like to find out who your Guide is? Maybe there's more than one!

- Go to your inner sacred space. (See Basic Meditation Exercise.)

- Ask to be open to receive information from your Guide.
- Know (believe) there is a Guide available to you at all times.
- Notice how the energy is already changing around you. Are you tingling? Do you feel a sense of anticipation and excitement?
- Close your eyes and imagine you are in a place where you feel comfortable. It could be a park. It could be your living room. Or it could be your front porch swing. You're there alone.
- Now, someone is approaching. Look at this person. Who is it? A male? A female? A group of people?
- How is this person dressed?
- Ask them their name or names. Go with your first impression. Again, go with your very first impression.
- Now ask them if they have a message for you. What do they have to say? Does this feel strange? Or does it feel like a reunion with someone you know very well?
- Spend time conversing with your guide or guides.
- After you have finished talking with them, thank them and invite them to return.
- Take a few deep breaths and ground yourself by doing something physical, such as cleaning house or eating something.

- You might want to write about your experience. Remember to include the date and time.

After you have completed this exercise, think back about the Guide you contacted. Perhaps, as a child, you always had a fascination with Renaissance Italy. Was your Guide from that time period? Maybe you loved the history of Native Americans and the Guide who approached you was a Cherokee medicine woman.

Guides come from every walk of life. There is nothing particularly lofty about them. They were just people like you and I who have offered to help you on an as-called basis from The Other Side.

Earthbound Spirits

What are earthbound spirits?

We've all heard the stories about Anne Boleyn's head-toting apparition frightening people who dare to visit the Tower of London and the tale of old Mrs. Winchester who still wanders through her maze of a house.

Why have so many reported seeing these apparitions and why do spirits continue to linger on the earth plane?

Sometimes, these types of hauntings are caused by revenant energy imprinted like a photograph at a place. When people see these apparitions, they may be merely seeing an energy *movie* of an intensely charged event that happened there in the past.

But not all of these forms of hauntings are residual energy. Some are actually the spirits of the people who, for whatever reason, cannot let go of what happened to them and are repeating it eternally. They are blind to the outside world and are reliving events known to them.

Some spirits simply choose, for their own reasons, not to cross over to The Other Side. Some do not feel worthy. Some fear what will happen to them. People who have grown up believing in a vengeful god who will cast them into a fiery pit for their sins are not likely to want to go to The Other Side when they die.

A mother who dies prematurely, leaving behind a young family with no one to care for her children, is also unlikely to want to cross over. A father who left his struggling family with no insurance might want to cling to the earth plane and attempt to contact and help his loved ones.

We've all heard the term unfinished business. It's a very real thing to spirits.

Some mediums are of the opinion earthbound spirits are bad and they perform all manner of ritualistic ceremonies to chase them into the Light. Earthbound spirits are no more bad or good than they were here on earth. Their energy is not bad for you. It won't harm you to talk to them. It won't lower your energy or surround you with negative energy.

Rituals such as waving a sage smudge stick or lighting a white candle may make you feel as if you're connecting to the spirit world. However, you do not need anything outside yourself to connect with The Other Side or to guide a spirit into the Light.

Your *intention* is the power behind the ritual.

Rituals simply put a person in their own proper state of mind to connect with spirits. However, if your intention is to connect, then you will. No rituals needed.

If someone asks you to come to their house to "ghost bust" the previous owner who won't seem to leave, then do so as if the person were still alive and you were going to ask them why they persisted in staying long after their house was sold.

Politely and respectfully ask the lingering spirit why they are there and then explain to them that there is a better place for them.

Spirits still have all the emotions we have here on earth — only their feelings are intensified.

Be respectful. Treat the soul as you would want your soul to be treated.

At some point in your tenure as a medium, a spirit will ask you to help them cross over. It's a very simple process. Always ask to be certain the spirit is ready to make the transition. Spirits have free will. You cannot force a soul to leave who doesn't want to go.

What you can do is invite the spirit's loved ones on The Other Side to a sort of intervention. Ask them to join you in an attempt to explain to the spirit how wonderful things really are on The Other Side. When the spirit in question then, and only then, asks you to assist them in crossing over, then bless the spirit, ask for it to be released from the earth plane and then feel its energy become lighter and lighter as it transitions.

How to Assist a Spirit in Crossing Over

If a spirit approaches you and you feel it wants assistance in crossing over to The Other Side, it's a very simple, but rewarding process.

- Go to your inner sacred space. (See Basic Meditation Exercise.)

- Invite any other spirits who were close to the soul on earth to come from The Other Side and welcome them. These spirits can assist you by imparting firsthand explanations as to the benefits of crossing over to the soul you wish to help.

- Ask the spirit who wants to cross over if he is aware of these helpers. (The answer will invariably be yes but check to make sure.)

- Tell the spirit he is released from the earth plane and ask him to follow his welcoming committee into the Light.

- Feel the static energy dissipate and become light around you as the spirit makes the transition.

- If the spirit is reluctant to go, then give him an open invitation to approach you anytime he is ready and willing to go. In this event, remember, you have not failed. The spirit has free will. Always.

The Other Side

What is heaven and where is it?

Heaven is everywhere.

It is all around us.

Heaven is within us.

It is in every person, every rock, every tree, everything.

But what is it?

Simply — heaven is whatever we believe it to be.

Super psychic and medium James Van Praagh says our society seems too focused on the outside or what we see in the physical, disregarding what is within. Van Praagh suggests that all things are a product of our thoughts and our creativity. We create our world, including our heaven, based on our thoughts.

If we, as creative beings, focus on learning and getting to know ourselves from within, we will then see the world with a much clearer perspective.

Perhaps it is impossible for us to conceive of heaven while we are physical beings on the earth plane. But according to the Guides with whom I've communicated, when our bodies die and we pass into spirit, we are at once met on The Other Side by people and animals familiar to us. It is a joyful reunion.

Heaven is a place of great learning where we continue to grow spiritually.

I am often asked, "How can a spirit be here talking to us and be in heaven at the same time?"

It's easy. All religions have belief in a Creator who is omnipresent. If heaven is indeed within us, then so are all the souls who reside there. And if we are made in the image of the Creator, then we are also creative beings who are omnipresent souls.

We do not possess a soul. We are a soul.

According to quantum physics, whenever an event takes place or a decision is made in which there's a choice of possibilities, the universe divides so that every possibility is realized but in different dimensions. This means that an infinity of new universes are generated every instant. We ourselves theoretically exist in countless different dimensions, doing different things and thinking different thoughts. This particular brain of ours is only aware of one of these dimensions—this one.

Simply put, time and space do not exist in the spirit world. We are infinite beings. We have always been and always will be.

We create our own realities with our own beliefs.

Timelessness is a difficult thing for us to grasp because we think and live in a linear fashion but spirits are not aware of time on The Other Side.

Many psychics will tell you they are not good at predicting the time in which an event will happen. Often psychics will say something like, "I'm getting a *two* on this. By that, I mean it could be two weeks, two years, two months, two decades."

Why? Because spirits who pass along this information have lost their concept of linear time on The Other Side.

Since none of these theories can be proven, form your own opinion with the help of your Guides.

Exploring Your Heaven Exercise

- Go to your sacred inner space. (See Basic Meditation Exercise.)
- Take some time to think about what you hope heaven might be like.
- Visualize the heaven you have imagined. Use all your senses. What do you see? How do you feel? Are there fragrances? Is there food? What do you hear?
- After you explore your five senses, take it a step further and explore your psychic or sixth sense. What are you capable of knowing?
- How would you like heaven to be different from your preconceived notions? How would you like heaven to be similar?
- What and whom do you expect to see there? Are there people? Are there pets?
- Ask your Spirit Guide to show you images of heaven. Is it a place? Or is it here on earth? Do you see others there? Are there buildings? Or is there just brilliant white light?
- How does it make you feel to imagine heaven?

- Bring these good feelings back into your daily life with you.
- You might want to journal about your beliefs.
- Afterward, reground yourself to the physical world.

Laying the Foundation

As with building a house, becoming a medium also requires that you lay a solid foundation. Mediumship is an ongoing learning process. It is a discipline, like any other that requires practice to perfect.

Mediumship also requires a great deal of patience. As you work with your Guides and the exercises in this book, you will develop your mediumistic ability. Spirits tend to work with our needs and desires very quickly but spirits, especially your Guides, will only offer you information for which you are ready. Some abilities will come to you quickly. Other skills will take work and devoted practice.

A personal sense of integrity and knowing your own values is a must for anyone delving into mediumship.

Keeping an open mind — or being open to receive messages from spirits — is a necessity.

Your ability as a medium will increase both spiritually and with precision if you maintain a sense of humility along with compassion and empathy for yourself and others.

In becoming a medium, you will learn a great deal about yourself. Some of the exercises in this book will require you to explore and define your beliefs and self-truths.

You will become a link between our world and the spirit world with the ability to offer proof of the continued existence of the soul after the death of the physical body.

You will be able to tap into a higher consciousness and feel your connection to your Creator and to everything that makes up the Universe.

Becoming a medium is an exciting and rewarding journey!

Are you ready to get started?

Asking For Mediumistic Ability

The first step in becoming a medium is very simple.

Ask.

Ask the Universe, ask God, ask your Source — but ask. Put it out to the Universe that you want this ability.

There is no one way to ask for mediumship ability. But anytime you make a request to the Universe, think it through.

The Universe is ready, willing and able to provide you with your heart's desire. Remember Dorothy at the end of *The Wizard of Oz* when she realized the ruby slippers had provided her with the power to return to Kansas all along? If I'd been Dorothy, I would have been irate that the Good Witch of the North did not tell me the minute those shoes showed up on my feet.

Think about it. You know this as well. Regardless of what your core beliefs are, the Bible states a universal truth in Matthew 21:22 — "And all things, whatsoever ye shall ask in prayer, believing, ye shall receive."

But have you ever gotten what you wanted and then wished you hadn't?

Take some time to think through why you want to be a medium, what your expectations are and what you plan to do with it after it happens.

Exploring Your Motivation to Become a Medium Exercise

There is phenomenal power in the written word. If the Ten Commandments had simply been passed down orally instead of carved in stone, imagine the difference in the impact Moses would have made.

When an idea is written down, it takes on its own life. It holds permanent importance and is there for all to see.

The earliest civilizations realized this phenomenon as well. Even before there were written words, people recorded stories on the walls of caves.

The written word provides structure that oral statements do not. Writing out your thoughts can help you visualize the goals you would like to accomplish.

Give each of the questions below a few minutes of thought then write out your answers. The more detailed the better. Make up a list of questions you have about mediumship and write out the answers. You may be surprised at the end result.

- ❖ Why do you want to be a medium?
- ❖ What, exactly, do you want from mediumship ability?
- ❖ What do you hope to accomplish with mediumship ability?
- ❖ How can developing mediumship ability enhance your life? Take a

moment to visualize this. Feel the emotions associated with it.

❖ See yourself engaged in being a medium. How do you see others reacting to you? Are you helping others or do you use your ability to boost your own spirituality? Is this a positive visualization?

❖ Once again, feel all the emotions associated with the visualization.

❖ If all this seems right for you, then tell the Universe with conviction, "I want to be a medium."

❖ From now on, consider yourself a medium.

❖ Thank the Universe for providing this gift to the best of your ability.

Belief

Belief is not something you can develop through practice. At this point, you may not even really know what it is you believe. *The American Heritage Dictionary of the English Language*, Fourth Edition, defines "belief" as:

❖ The mental act, condition or habit of placing trust or confidence in another: My belief in you is as strong as ever.

- ❖ Mental acceptance of and conviction in the truth, actuality or validity of something: His explanation of what happened defies belief.
- ❖ Something believed or accepted as true, especially a particular tenet or a body of tenets accepted by a group of persons.

My first encounter with a spirit happened in 2001, after I bought Martin Piano Company, a sixty-year-old business. The former owner, Ryan Martin, died of a heart attack in the store on February 5, 1957, nine years before I was born.

I spent my days at the business, for the most part, alone.

Oddly enough, people who spend inordinate amounts of time alone seem to be more ripe for psychic development than the average person. There's nothing magical about loners. However, they are usually people who are introspective and, for whatever reason, are comfortable turning within for answers.

Luke 17:20–21 states: 20 "And being asked by the Pharisees, when the kingdom of God cometh, he answered them and said, The kingdom of God cometh not with observation:" 21 "neither shall they say, Lo, here! or, There! for lo, the kingdom of God is within you."

This may sound simplistic but this is exactly where spirits communicate with us. *Within.*

Spirits communicate by blending their knowledge, their energy and their consciousness with the living to form coherent images, words and messages.

Having not known this little truism at the time, it must have been very difficult for Ryan to communicate with me. Shortly after I began working at Martin Piano, I had a number of experiences that I considered the usual ghostly stuff. I heard footsteps made by an unseen person and caught the smells of cigarettes and cigars when no one smoked in the business. An occasional whiff of Old Spice mingled with the distinct scent of Clubman barber's talc wafted my way. I felt the cliché cold drafts and witnessed doors opening and closing.

These are the type of things that can be dismissed easily enough and, if you talk too much about it, earn you some time on a therapist's couch. However, the feeling I had that someone was there—standing nearby—watching me was a little harder to dismiss.

I wondered. But I did not know. Like most sane people, I explained the occurrences away.

After about six months of Ryan's classic haunting *modus operandi*, he made his presence irrefutably known to me by introducing himself audibly. He simply said, "Hello."

Although I was initially startled, I was intrigued enough to form a tenuous friendship with him.

Still, the development of my ability did not happen overnight. I knew Ryan was present. Or rather, I had a *strong feeling* Ryan was present. At the time, I kept expecting an appearance or even to hear his voice again.

I felt as if I were imagining what his favorite color was or which baseball team he followed. I felt he enjoyed my presence in the store but I constantly wondered if I was wrong.

At that time, I had no idea whether or not what my intuition picked up was correct. I did not trust my own insight. I did not trust my own judgment. I'd spent a good many years ignoring my intuition. Therefore, learning to trust the impressions I received from Ryan — the voice that came from within — *that* was very difficult for me to grasp. I doubted it. I feared it.

I believe that these feelings are common to all people who choose to develop psychic and mediumistic skills at some point in their lives, especially for those of us who weren't born rattling off predictions and channeling spirits.

I consulted a local psychic, a very gifted woman whose expertise was in giving fast, to-the-point readings. She confirmed Ryan's presence for me and thus, I discovered the second step in becoming a medium.

Belief.

Although I had my doubts about my ability, I truly believed there was an intelligent entity sharing my space who wished to communicate with me. After all, he had said, "hello".

Your Beliefs Exercise

Take out a pen and paper and define the terms listed below according to your own beliefs. Please don't write what you think others expect you to write or copy from the dictionary. Your beliefs are your own and all your beliefs are valid. There are no wrong answers. I simply want you to get in touch with what you believe—with what you feel.

With so many belief systems and opinions being impressed on us from outside sources—magazines, television, politicians, church leaders, the Internet—it is sometimes difficult to get in touch with our own core beliefs. It is important to define what *you* believe so you can work within those parameters on your quest to developing mediumship.

It is not necessary for you to change your values or beliefs, only for you to recognize them.

These writing exercises should be thought-provoking. Don't worry about crossing all your t's and dotting all the i's. This is just a guide for you and your spiritual development. If you chose to read for others, you will be asked what spiritual beliefs you hold. It will be important for you to have an answer ready. In addition, becoming conscious of your own beliefs will help you interpret messages from spirits for yourself and others.

That said, what beliefs come to mind as you read the following terms?

❖ Soul
❖ Spirit

❖ Life
❖ Death
❖ The Afterlife
❖ The Universe/Heaven/God/Creator

The following questions may help you to fine-tune your personal definitions of the above:

❖ What experiences formed your opinions and beliefs about Heaven, a Creator, the Afterlife?

❖ How has your Creator worked in your life?

❖ What makes you believe in this Creator?

❖ What miracles have you witnessed large or small?

❖ Think of a time your prayers or requests were answered. How did this make you feel?

❖ Think of a time your prayers or requests were answered in an unexpected way.

❖ Think of a time when your prayers or requests were not answered and you saw how the Universe was working to protect you. What insight or lessons did you learn from this experience?

❖ What are your beliefs about mediumship, about speaking to spirits?
❖ How does mediumship fit in with your core spiritual beliefs?

Take your time with those questions. Give it some thought and write everything down. Leave plenty of room to come back and add more later.

Don't feel guilty if your beliefs aren't what you see or hear from others.

Beliefs can change over time. Be open to your own thoughts. Listen to your feelings. Write from your heart. No one else has to read what you write so feel free to expound and explore your own beliefs.

Expectations

We are often oblivious to spirit communication because we expect it to happen the way we communicate as living, breathing souls in bodies. Our expectations of what it is actually like to communicate with a spirit can set us up for disappointment.

Communicating with spirits is not what you've seen in the movies. You're probably not going to be confiding in Bruce Willis that you "see dead people". When John Edward or Sylvia Browne tell you they hear a voice, they're not talking about an audible voice.

They are referring to that *inner voice* we all have.

Spirits do not have bodies so they use what they do have to contact us — thought energy.

Be Open to Receive

Whenever I communicated with Ryan, he encouraged me to open my mind to receive. I had no idea what he meant until I found a book entitled *Open Your Mind to Receive* by Catherine Ponder. In it, she explains that our thoughts are often roadblocks to receiving the good the Universe wants us to have. However, the eye opener for me was how Ponder explained that we should not fix our thoughts on one outcome.

This theory holds true when opening to receive information from The Other Side. Be open to what spirits have to say because you may receive unexpected information. This goes back to expectations again.

Remember to expect the unexpected.

Spirits can only work with what we know and what we can conceive. Spirits communicate through thought energy.

When we speak with spirits on The Other Side, thought energy assimilates with ours and *voila*, we have communication from spirits — but with our own spin on it.

Simply put, spirits can only use what we know in order to communicate with us. If you are a doctor who is well versed in medical terminology, then you can communicate with a spirit who also knows a lot of medical terminology. If I tried to communicate with such a spirit, it would be like trying to watch a foreign movie without the English subtitles.

Summary

After you have decided you want to develop your innate mediumistic ability and have explored your beliefs about mediumship and your expectations of mediumship, you are ready to begin accessing the wonderful knowledge that lies within you.

While you explore the spirit world, you will learn much about yourself. In turn, your life will be enriched. Your faith will increase. You will find you are a much more open and tolerant individual and you will realize your connectedness to God and The Universe.

❖ Ask
❖ Believe
❖ Expect the unexpected
❖ Be open to receive

Matthew 7:7 — Ask, and it shall be given you; seek, and ye shall find; knock, and it shall be opened unto you.

Energy Recognition

For the most part, energy, in and of itself, is something we cannot see. We know it's there. We know it works when we press a remote button or flip a light switch. But we can't see it, hold it, smell it, taste it or hear it.

So how do we believe in something that defies our five senses? We know conducted energy results in some sort of display of its power. We've all had experience with this. Right? When you flip a light switch, provided you've paid your utility bill, the light comes on. We rarely give it any more thought than that. When you turn on the radio, you hear live voices coming through your speaker. You can't see electricity or hear radio waves. But you do experience their results.

We know from quantum physicists that energy can neither be created nor destroyed. It simply changes form.

So it is with our consciousness after death. It simply changes from being housed in a body to being without a body.

How do we communicate with someone who has no body with which to produce a voice, gestures, a written word or even give us a glance?

The subtle ways living people communicate with each other are boundless. Spirits do not have that luxury. And neither do we as mediums.

Certainly spirits can get our attention by concentrating energy to move objects and even to create a voice but, as I understand it, the aforementioned ways of getting our attention are merely that. Think of it like a child acting up just to get mommy or daddy's attention. Whether the results are what the child intended, the child will get attention.

It takes a very concentrated amount of stored-up energy to create a noise or to utter a word and especially to form a full-fledged apparition. I'm not one of those who see dead people. Not with my eyes anyway. However, I do see them in my head—within. This is because I have developed my awareness.

When I first became aware of Ryan's presence, I felt it as static energy. It was the kind of energy that raises the fine hairs on your arms or makes the tip of your nose tingle. It was an energy I had to learn to feel.

Begin to notice how a living person's energy feels to you. Have you ever paid attention to how it feels good to be around certain people and bad to be around others? Notice how the energy affects you.

Become aware.

Pay attention to how it feels when someone you love comes within three feet of you. You may feel warmth and excitement. This energy is good and you might liken it to soft velvet.

Next time someone you don't like invades your personal space, notice the change in feeling. You immediately want to cross your arms to block an energy exchange. You may shudder and recoil. This energy feels static. Sandpapery.

Spirit energy will feel similar. Some spirits will feel good to you and some might feel uncomfortable. Use your own discretion. You are always in control. If you have a bad feeling, politely ask the spirit to leave.

Recognizing Energy Exercise 1

- Rub your hands together vigorously and then hold them an inch apart.
- Hold them closer without touching and then pull them farther apart.
- Repeat, moving your hands toward and away from each other until you can feel the very subtle changes in energy. You might feel it right away or it might take some practice. But eventually, you will feel it.

With a partner

- Hold your hand a few inches away from your partner's hand and feel his or her energy.
- Move your hands away from each other and then closer together without touching hands.
- Notice the subtle changes and fluctuations in energy. As you move your hands closer and away you may feel something akin to moving two magnets apart and closer together. Pay attention to the energy vibrations.

- Don't be discouraged if you don't feel anything at first. Keep practicing. Energy is something you must learn to recognize and feel.

Recognizing Energy Exercise 2

- Hold your hand close to a computer screen, television screen and a speaker, all of which are turned on.
- What do you feel?
- How does the feel of the energy differentiate from the computer screen to the speaker?
- Feel the energy of the TV screen.
- Step away and try to re-create it with the hand rubbing exercise.
- Take notice when you are alone and you feel that subtle little tingle.
- Is there a spirit close by?
- Ask your Spirit Guide or someone you know who is in spirit to come close to you.
- Feel the energy.

Recognizing Energy Exercise 3

- Get a deck of regular playing cards.

- Take out five red cards and five black cards.
- Get still and quiet and take a couple of deep breaths.
- Ask to be open to receive.
- Hold one of the red cards and feel the energy of red. Colors have vibrations, and yes, they also have their own energy.
- Feel and be aware of your *connection* to the colors, the cards and the Universe.
- Now put your red card back in your deck of ten and shuffle them.
- Face down, take one card at a time and feel the vibrations. Does the card feel red or black?
- Go with your first instinct.

How many did you get right? The odds are, provided you did not guess red every time, you'll get three right. I'll bet you did better than the odds and, if you keep up the practice, you might even get all ten!

Discernment

Since you will be using your sixth sense instead of your five physical senses to communicate with The Other Side, how will you be able to tell one spirit from another?

I have several friends who developed their gifts as mediums. All of them, including me, had to learn the skill of discerning one spirit from another.

In the beginning, all spirit energy felt alike to me. It was just energy. It made me tingle all over, break out in gooseflesh and raised the hairs on my arms. I couldn't tell if I was talking to Ryan or to my Grandma Dollie.

When you open up to receive information from those in spirit, verify who it is by asking one or two questions of confirmation.

"Did you have blue eyes?"

"Did you have two children?"

Spirits with an urgent message tire of this form of testing pretty quickly. Keep your discernment questions short and to the point.

If you don't get confirmation from the spirit immediately and choose not to pursue a conversation with the spirit who has approached you, then thank the spirit for stopping by and ask it to move on. Be firm but courteous. You are always in control.

Pay attention to the feeling you get from the spirit. Is it a good feeling? How does your body react? Anytime you receive the impression the source is not a good one, thank the spirit for coming, bless it and request that it move on.

Be open to the possibility that someone totally unexpected to you may approach. Spirits recognize our *openness* to communicate with them. The spirit who has come to you may have a message for someone else!

Always use your own judgment. Never base decisions solely on information you receive from The Other Side. Get in tune with your body and use discretion to make decisions that are in your best interest.

Also realize that your Guides will offer you plenty of opportunities to learn to recognize spirit energy. You may have the feeling you aren't getting any good information but you are! You are learning the very valuable lesson of discernment.

Discernment will help you tremendously when you start reading for others.

You can only learn discernment through practice.

When you are a strong, well-balanced person, then you will attract like spirits.

Discernment Exercise

This exercise will require you to enlist the help of two different spirits and your pendulum. (See Pendulum Exercise in Tools section.)

- Go to your inner sacred space. (See Basic Meditation Exercise.)
- Call on your Spirit Guide and also ask for the help of someone you knew who is now on The Other Side.
- Charge your pendulum and then suspend it loosely from your fingers.
- Ask your Guide to move the pendulum.

- Don't ask questions at this point. Just feel this energy that is unique to your Guide.
- After you've spent a minute or two soaking up your Guide's energy, ask your spirit friend to come through and move the pendulum.
- Spend a few minutes feeling this energy.
- Alternate back and forth between your Guide and your spirit loved one.
- How do the energies differ? The Guide's energy may feel finer or faster to you. Your spirit loved one's energy may feel a little stronger. You might get a little shiver up your spine when you focus on feeling these two different energies.
- Practice this until you are able to recognize the difference between your Guide and your spirit loved one.

Recognizing energy is one of the more challenging aspects of mediumship to develop. However, if you keep up your practice, you will soon be able to tell whether spirits are male, female, Guides or relatives, and the association to you or others. Coupling your instincts with your practice will make your readings accurate and amazing!

Communicating with The Other Side

Communicating with spirits is easier than you might think. The difficulty comes from our own self-doubt. With practice, you can learn to trust your intuition and the information you receive from spirits.

Whenever you choose to interact with the spirit who has come to communicate with you, first find out what message they have for you.

Sample Questions

- ❖ Are you here with a message for me?
- ❖ Is it about career?
- ❖ Family?
- ❖ Finances?
- ❖ Spiritual development?
- ❖ Health?

There are several different types of mediumistic abilities. The exercises in this book involve many different ones, sometimes two or three at a time! Try them all and find which technique works best for you.

I am clairsentient and clairaudient. Clairvoyance is more difficult for me although sometimes it comes across as a strength.

You may be primarily clairvoyant, which relies on the mind's eye, however during a reading, another sense may take over. For instance, you might taste brownies and when you report this impression your client remarks their loved one in spirit's favorite food was brownies.

Some mediums even report experiencing panic attacks before something bad happens or feeling nauseated by particularly intense impressions from spirits.

Most people have two types of mediumistic abilities at which they excel but just because you are more comfortable with one or two, do not dismiss the others. How you receive the information also depends on what the spirits want to impart to you. Spirits have their strengths as well.

Learn which technique works best for you!

Types of Mediumistic Communication

Clairalience (Clear-smelling)	The ability to pick up a scent from a spirit, such as recognizing a spirit's cologne or favorite flower
Clairaudience (Clear-hearing)	Hearing messages from spirits, either internally or externally; the ability to pick up names and phrases or specific words
Claircognizance (Clear-knowing)	When a thought simply pops into your mind
Clairgustance (Clear-tasting)	The ability to receive taste impressions from a spirit
Clairsentience (Clear-feeling)	Gut feelings or hunches
Clairvoyance (Clear-seeing)	Seeing symbols, shapes, people, places or situations in your *mind's eye* or with your physical eyes

Quick Information Exercise

- Go to your inner sacred space. (See Basic Meditation Exercise.)
- Invite your Spirit Guide to communicate with you.
- Ask your Guide to tap your teeth together gently, once for "yes" answers, twice for "no" answers and three times for "don't know" or "maybe" answers.
- When you have finished your communication, thank your Guide.
- Reground by eating, going for a walk and so on.

You will soon be able to quickly get into a relaxed state to use this discreet form of spirit communication anywhere!

Communication Exercise

- Go to your inner sacred space. (See Basic Meditation Exercise.)
- Think of someone on The Other Side, preferably someone you loved whose presence made you happy. Hint: Trying to contact famous dead people doesn't work all that well. John Lennon is about as likely to talk to you now as he would have been

when he was alive if you had just called him up on the phone and expected him to converse with you.

- Remember the person you chose to contact. Information you obtain using your fledgling ability will feel very much like remembering something—a feeling, a sound, a smell, an experience. Use all your senses in remembering them.

- Now, how does it feel around you?

- Take this memory a step further. If that person about whom you're thinking could talk to you, what would they be saying? Take some time with this one.

- What would a conversation be like between you? Sit and enjoy reconnecting with this person. Don't ask advice at this point. Simply visit and enjoy your spirit friend's company.

- After you've conversed, invite them to join you again, thank them for coming, give them a hug or whatever comes naturally.

- Take a few deep breaths and reconnect to this world. Eat something, enjoy a bath or a shower, take a walk or bike ride. Do something that will ground you in the physical world.

- You may want to reflect on this experience by writing it down in a journal or notebook. Include the date and the time along with the message you received from your spirit friend.

Congratulations! If you did this exercise, I have no doubt you made contact with the spirit world!

That seems far too simple, doesn't it? You probably felt as if you were making it all up. That's perfect, because that's what it is supposed to feel like.

Communication with those on The Other Side will often feel as if you are *making it up*. But soon, provided you continue to practice this exercise, you will receive something called *validation*. Validation is when the messages you receive from a spirit are confirmed for you in the physical world.

When I first began talking with Ryan, I asked him what his mother's name was. I picked up the name *Patrick*. At first, I thought I was wrong. Patrick is certainly not a woman's name.

However, a local genealogist found a census report with Ryan's mother's name on it. Mary Patrick Martin.

My message from Ryan was validated.

Can Spirits Predict the Future?

Can a spirit predict your future? Maybe. Remember what I told you about the personality not changing on The Other Side? Well, that also holds true for asking spirits to give you advice about the future.

Suppose you are communicating with your Uncle Elmer who was a successful Wall Street wizard. Since the personality holds true even after we pass into spirit, Uncle Elmer would probably be a good source of information if you were interested in trading stocks. However, if Uncle Elmer was a gambler who gasped his last breath on the floor of a casino after losing the deed to the farm in a poker game, then you might be wary of asking him for any sort of financial advice.

If you are reading for a client and they ask, "When will that special person come into my life?" or "When will I win the lottery?", it would be wise to educate your client about how to use their own power of creativity to bring about what they want in their lives.

Spirits are not magical beings who are going to right all our wrongs and give us the Powerball numbers.

When you are consulting The Other Side about future endeavors, always tag on this little phrase: "Is this in my best interest?"

Otherwise, you might receive confusing information.

Also remember that we are creatures who have been given the gift of free will. The future is not set in stone but rather it is a series of paths to choose and take.

Spirits are more than willing to help guide you. But you have to ask the right question the right way in order to get the right answer. Just remember to add, "Would this be in my best interest?"

Prediction Exercise

- Think of a question you have about a future endeavor.
- Close your eyes and take a few deep breaths. Get relaxed.
- Go to your inner sacred space. (See Basic Meditation Exercise.)
- Feel your connection to the Universe and to all that is.
- Now imagine yourself in a peaceful place. A park. A front porch swing. Lying on the beach.
- Ask for a visit from a Spirit Guide who has advice for you on this subject.
- Someone approaches you and you recognize this person as your Spirit Guide.
- Simply feel the presence. It is not necessary to know their name or see their features. Just know this person is there for you and it is someone you can trust.
- Pose your question. An example might be something like this: Would it be in my best interest to buy a new car at this time?
- Be very specific. *Is it in my best interest to _____ or to _____?* If you don't get an answer right away, imagine yourself in the situation about which you are asking.

- If you asked about buying a new car, imagine yourself purchasing this car.
- Now imagine yourself not buying a car. Think it through.
- How does each situation feel?
- What does your Spirit Guide have to say?
- What images do you get?
- What physical reactions does your body give you?
- Listen with your whole self.

Again, you might feel as if you are making this up but by tagging "Is this in my best interest?" to your question, you are guaranteed to get in touch with your subconscious and obtain the answers that are right for you.

Imparting Information from Spirit to Others

How do you approach someone with a message you've obtained from The Other Side? Most of us won't have huge audiences of people lined up to hear what messages we have to relay to them from the spirit world like John Edward or Sylvia Browne.

It's much more likely that you'll be approached by spirits the way Jennifer Love Hewitt is in *Ghost Whisperer*.

When you open up to other dimensions, you cast out a beacon that attracts spirits to you.

This very thing happened to me.

Right before bed one night, my husband and I heard someone walking upstairs. We were so convinced it was a living someone, he armed himself and headed up the stairs. I grabbed the phone and had my finger ready to punch 9-1-1. A thorough investigation of the house turned up no one.

During the night, our shower door opened and closed. Footsteps could be heard scuffling along the carpet, right next to the bed. Finally around 4:00 a.m., I asked Ryan, "Who is that?"

Instantly, my mind flew to Mike, my hubby's business partner's dad who'd recently died unexpectedly. I mentally told Mike I'd talk to him in the morning and asked him if he'd please be quiet so I could get some sleep. He complied.

The next morning, my husband told me, "You know, I think that was Mike last night."

I immediately sat down to communicate with him through automatic writing, which is a form of spirit communication. Automatic writing is performed in either a slight or deep trance state and is similar to free writing in that the process or writing produced is not derived from conscious thought.

Mike wrote that he wanted me to help him talk to his daughter, Linda. Linda knows about my mediumship ability because she previously contacted me about getting a message from an ancestor her family had actually seen in her home. But this was a totally different scenario. Mike had died only two months before. Linda and her family were still in shock and grieving. How could I tell them Mike had followed my husband home and had given us such cause for alarm that we searched the house for an intruder?

I knew I had to handle the situation delicately. I took a chance and emailed Linda. I told her I'd been contacted by a spirit I felt might be Mike and asked her if she'd like me to see what he had to say.

Shortly afterward, I received an email from her saying that she'd felt compelled to call me and was pleasantly surprised to get my email. She dearly wanted me to talk to Mike. At that point, I sent her his messages.

The reading was accurate and validating for Linda and her family.

But not all of my anecdotes are success stories. Once I was asked to do table tipping for a group of ladies. Table tipping is a technique that was started by the Spiritualists in the last half of the nineteenth century. Sitters position themselves around a lightweight card table, place their hands lightly on top and invite spirits to communicate. The spirits then *speak* by lifting the table onto two legs and tapping out answers by tapping once for "yes" and twice for "no". (See Table Tipping section for further details.)

Gina, the lady who called, was very open to it. She'd tabled with me before. She wanted to bring along her five sisters so I assumed they were all open to it as well.

I was mistaken.

At once, the table lifted. I felt it was the spirit of their grandfather. He confirmed that by tapping once. I asked him mentally for his name. He told me and I reported it to the ladies. Initially, the women were in awe but since several of them were not prepared to receive the message from their grandfather, one of the sisters accused me of hiring a private investigator to tell me the names of their deceased relatives so I could hoodwink them.

It is rewarding to give readings that help others and also validate your ability but don't set yourself up to be ridiculed or chastised. Not everyone wants to believe spirits are happy and willing to communicate with us on this side.

Talking to spirits can be lighthearted but it can also be serious business. Don't rush out to tell a mother who has just lost her eight-year-old son he has a message for her.

However, if you feel you have a valid message from a persistent spirit who insists you give it to someone, ask your Guides and the Universe to set it up so that you will feel comfortable imparting the information.

Automatic Writing Exercise

- After you've practiced the exercise on feeling energy, get a fluid writing ink pen and a notebook.
- Go to your inner sacred space. (See Basic Meditation Exercise.)
- Ask to be open to receive.
- Summon your Gatekeeper and request that only spirits who have your best interest at

heart be allowed to communicate with you.

- Put the pen to the paper, relax your hand and your elbow and just let it write.
- Ask questions. The more specific your question, the better the response you will receive.
- When you are finished, thank the spirits who communicated with you and thank your Guides for their protection.
- Reground by eating something, taking a walk, taking a bath, anything that puts you back in touch with the physical world.

Some people refer to automatic writing as free writing. When you automatic write, don't think. Just do it. At first, the pen might make scribbles. That's okay. The spirits are learning to combine their energy with yours, to use you as a channel. And yes, this is a form of channeling.

You are a conduit or channel for spirit energy. Spirits rarely come in, take over and start babbling out of your mouth. If you're concerned about it happening to you, ask your Gatekeeper Guide to prevent that. The spirits know your limits and are more than happy to work within your boundaries.

Remember, you are always in control. And remember to relax your hand and just let it go. You might feel a tingling sensation or your hand might get very cold or very warm. The sensation differs for everyone.

This, like all the other exercises with spirits, takes practice.

Ask your Spirit Guide to come in and write. Notice the energy difference when you write with the spirit of someone you knew in life and when you write with a Guide.

Practice, practice, practice! Have fun. When you start getting coherent words, ask The Other Side for information you can validate.

Things to Keep in Mind when Communicating with Spirits

❖ Do not entertain entities who don't give you a good feeling. Politely ask them to leave or to move into the Light. Ask the Universe to bless them. Never show anger. If you do not feel you are getting good information, end the communication. (As stated before, avoid the use of alcohol and drugs during any spirit contact.)

❖ Be patient with yourself and your spirit friends. Both of you are likely learning a new skill.

❖ Remember that the personality remains constant after death. Some spirits are serious while others like to joke. Approach them as you would have in life.

❖ The best messages come through when higher level questions are asked. Example: *What can I do to make myself more spiritually aware?* or *How can I increase my psychic awareness?* Questions that are not always answered are more base in nature, such as, *Can you give me next week's lottery numbers?*

❖ Not all spirits can give information about the future and you should be extremely cautious with the information if they do. Ultimately, this is your life and the choices you make should be based on your own feelings and intuition. Spirits are here to guide us, not to make decisions for us. Never rely solely on messages from spirits.

❖ The old adage "if the spirit is willing" is a truism in the business of speaking to disincarnate souls. The spirit itself has to believe communication is possible and that it is in everyone's best interest to do so.

❖ The personality doesn't change when someone dies. If Uncle Elmer was a fun-loving cut-up on the earth plane, he'll be a fun-loving cut-up on The Other Side. If he was a misanthrope, then don't expect any sort of reformation or enlightenment just because he passed into spirit.

Symbology

Symbols are universally—and spiritually— understood.

Since spirit communication comes through thought energy, if the spirits who work with you know in advance that certain symbols have meaning to you, they can relay information much more quickly and accurately without you having to interpret.

That's why super mediums like John Edward use a symbols list. If you have watched his show *Crossing Over*, then you have heard him say, "This spirit is showing me pink roses. That's my symbol for love."

In essence, John Edward has given the spirits— and himself—a nifty cheat sheet. He has laid out his rules of communication up front so both he and the spirits with which he communicates know what to expect and how to deliver the information in a way John will understand.

You can do this as well and make it infinitely easier to communicate with The Other Side.

Symbols Exercise

Think of some symbols that have meaning to you. Do you equate a dove with peace? When you see a woman dressed in white does a bride or a wedding come to mind? Think of some universal symbols. A red hexagon means stop. An inverted yellow triangle signifies caution. An eye or even an owl might stand for knowledge.

Think of the questions which you would ask spirits. What do you want to know? Finances? Health? Love?

The possibilities are endless.

And the symbols you choose will vary from the symbols someone else would use depending on what information and guidance you wish to glean from those in spirit.

As you make your own list, be creative!

Making Your Own Symbols List Exercise

- You will need a notebook or journal you plan to keep and a pen.

- Make a list of concepts based on information you want your Guide or spirit friends to impart to you. For example: finances, health, travel, career, love, past, present, future, warning, time. Add anything else to your list you choose!

- Now, think of symbols for each item on your list. Make your symbol something simple that your Guide can show you. For example: You might equate finances with a bag of money or a treasure chest. Your symbol for health could be a stethoscope. Travel could be signified by a ship or an airplane. You can get more specific after you practice with basic symbols. For example: If you have a ship next to travel on your list, you could ask your Guide for more specific means of travel by putting an automobile, a ship, an airplane, a bicycle — whatever you want!

- When reading for others, simply mentioning what the symbol signifies to you is usually enough information. Often, it's best to leave the interpretation of your symbols up to the person for whom you are doing a reading.

- You can always return to your list later to create more detailed symbols or to add new ones. Developing mediumship is an ongoing growth process!

Practicing with Symbols Exercise

- Each morning go to your inner sacred space. (See Basic Meditation Exercise.)
- Practice receiving symbol messages by asking your Guide to show you a symbol that will have relevance to your day.
- Write down the symbol you are shown.
- At the end of your day, write out how knowing about the issue helped or prepared you.

The more you practice working with symbols with your Guide, the better both you and your Guide will get at using them to make your readings fast and precise!

Accepted Universal Symbols

Change	Creek
Death	Tombstone
Fertility	Rabbit
Finances, good	Bag of gold
Finances, bad	Empty bag
Future	Three cards in a line with emphasis on the right
Health	Caduceus or Wand of Hermes, which depicts two snakes wound around a winged staff
Love	Pink roses
Military	Flag
Past	Three cards in a line with emphasis on the left
Present	Three cards in a line with emphasis on the middle
Prosperity	Sun
Spirituality	Cross or other symbol one personally relates to spirituality/religion
Stability	Rock
Time	Clock or calendar
Travel	Airplane

Dreams

During rapid eye movement sleep, images and feelings surface in our subconscious, which we refer to as dreams.

Everybody dreams whether they remember their dreams or not.

The dream state is one of the least understood areas of human phenomena and yet it is one of the most highly debated among psychologists.

The study of the science of dreams is called oneirology. According to *Brain Basics: Understanding Sleep*, a study conducted by the National Institute of Neurological Disorders and Stroke, the average human spends about six years of life dreaming. That is an average of two hours per night.

Throughout time, people have searched for meanings in their dreams. The ancient Greeks believed dream symbols could be used for healing and also divine inspiration. Early psychologists Sigmund Freud and Carl Jung believed dreams were merely an interaction between the conscious and the unconscious. Others held that dreams were a part of the human psyche the dreamer sought to repress.

Aside from offering insight into our subconscious mind, dreams are one of the most common ways spirits can communicate with us. Think back over dreams you've had in the past that involved seeing a deceased friend or relative. In the dream, you knew the person had passed and yet you talked and interacted with them as if they were still with you on the earth plane.

Dreams of people who have passed into spirit are usually very vivid and signify a *visitation* from your loved ones to you in your subconscious.

When we sleep and dream, the filters that prevent psychic information from entering our minds during day are not present. Spirits often find it easier to communicate with us during a dream state.

Such visitation dreams can be very comforting but they can also be full of meaning.

Remembering your dreams can prove difficult but there are ways to learn to increase dream recall.

Start by reminding yourself, throughout the day, that you will remember your dreams.

One way to ensure you remember your dreams is to create a dream journal.

Dream journals can be as elaborate or as simple as you choose. You can invest in a hardback journal at your local bookstore or you can use a notebook. It doesn't matter.

A dream journal can help you recall your dreams and it can also help you analyze your own dreams!

There are many ways to record your dreams.

Place your journal next to your bed and record dreams upon awakening. When you move large muscle groups such as your legs or trunk, you are more likely to forget your dreams.

If you cannot record your dream immediately, lie very still and go back over the details of your dream in your mind.

Associate the details with memories from the previous day. What triggered your dream? What did you eat the day before? Association will help you recall dreams more vividly.

You can either write down or sketch images you remember from your dreams in your dream journal.

After you have collected several dreams, look for common themes. Look for recurring dreams. Categorize your dreams by theme for easier analysis.

You can consult a dream dictionary but you have the innate ability to find meaning relevant to your life in your dreams.

Once you begin to notice common themes in your dreams, you can begin to influence your dream life.

If, for example, you often dream of cats, you can remind yourself during the day that when you see a cat in the dream state, that you are dreaming. When you begin to realize, within a dream, that you are dreaming, you can then begin to direct your dreams!

This is a wonderful way to make contact with The Other Side.

During the day, meditate on your guides and loved ones on The Other Side and invite them to visit you in your dreams. Spend a few moments thinking of things you'd like to say to them or do with them. Think of questions to which you'd like to know the answers.

Your spirit friends will know what to do.

Dream Exercise

- After you lie down at night, think of a loved one who is in spirit.
- Imagine this person with all your senses. How did they look, smell, feel? What did their voice sound like? What emotions did you experience when they were near?
- Invite your spirit loved one to visit you in your dreams.
- Look forward to connecting with him or her in your dream.
- Always ask your Spirit Guide to help you remember your dream.
- When you awaken from your dream state, lie still and recall every detail of your dream you possibly can. Often dream imagery is symbolic. For example, if you meditated on your grandfather who was a hardworking man during his lifetime, you might see a horse or an elephant in your dream. Your mind makes unconscious associations of which you might not be aware! Focus on the emotions rather than literal images.
- Record your visitation dreams in a dream journal including what impressions you received and especially your emotions about connecting with your spirit friends. You can sketch a picture of your dream or

you can write out the details. It's up to you! Enjoy and have fun.

- Look back over the dreams you've recorded from time to time and look for common themes.

Tools

The use of tools is widely debated among mediums. My experience with tools, such as pendulums, Ouija boards, tables, dowsing rods and so on, has been good. However, I rarely feel the need to use a tool anymore.

Spirits prefer to talk to you directly. It is the easiest way for them to come through. The tools are merely for those of us on this side of the veil who want some sort of validation so we don't feel like we're making up what we receive from The Other Side.

Tools are also great for giving your ability a jump start but eventually you will want to learn to communicate directly with spirits.

Like attracts like is one of the spiritual laws of the Universe. We see others through our perception of ourselves. When we see good in others, we are seeing the good we recognize and admire within ourselves. Conversely, when others evoke anger, greed or other negative emotions in us, we are seeing traits about ourselves we either wish to repress or deny.

The people we attract mirror our own personalities.

Not only do we attract living people into our lives whose energy matches our own, we also attract spirits whose energy is similar. If you are a good, positive person, who has a firm grasp on your beliefs and values, then you are going to attract like-minded spirits.

When we use a tool such as a Ouija board, a table, automatic writing or even a pendulum, we are inviting or attracting spirits to us.

Keeping the law of attraction in mind, it's a good idea to only work with spirits when you are feeling good and are in a good frame of mind.

Know you are divinely protected and safe. If a spirit approaches you about whom you don't have a good feeling or want to get to know, for whatever reason, just politely ask it to leave. Like unwanted guests, unwelcome spirits won't stay long if you don't entertain them.

Everyone has a Spirit Guide or team of Guides, whether you are aware of them or not (see "Spirit Guides" section), who will act on your behalf to protect you from unwelcome spirits.

Besides assisting with communication, using tools like the pendulum or the Ouija board, or techniques like table tipping, are great ways to learn to feel energy.

Use your own judgment when selecting a tool. If the Ouija board doesn't feel right to you, don't use it. But if you love the way the energy pulses through your hand and you get great information through it, by all means, enjoy it!

The Pendulum

The use of the pendulum is a simple technique in which the medium holds a pendant suspended from a chain or ribbon and invites spirits to spin it one direction for "yes" answers and another for "no" answers.

Pendulums are also used in dowsing and can be used to dowse maps to find hidden or buried items, underground water or mineral deposits. The pendulum can also be used by medical intuitives to diagnose health problems.

Pendulum Exercise

- Go to your inner sacred space. (See Basic Meditation Exercise.)
- Hold your pendulum in the palm of your hand for a few minutes and imagine your energy flowing into it. This will *charge* the pendulum and prepare it to work with you.
- Curl the chain around one of your fingers a couple of times so that the pendant dangles freely.
- Place your elbow on a solid surface.
- Call on your Gatekeeper and know this powerful spirit is there to protect you.
- Ask to receive energy from The Other Side to set the pendant in motion. Some people will see the pendulum swing in circles. Others may notice it vibrating vigorously or it may merely swing back and forth.
- Watch what happens. Be patient. It will start slowly at first, but the more you work

with The Other Side and the more spirits work with you, the quicker the pendulum will respond for you.

- Up the ante by asking the spirit to move the pendant one way for "yes" answers and another way for "no".
- Now, ask it "yes" and "no" questions.

This takes a little practice so don't get discouraged if the pendulum only vibrates or makes small motions. Soon you will be receiving answers telepathically before the pendulum is set in motion.

Dowsing

The technique of dowsing has been around for many years and has existed in many different forms. The most common form is known as water-witching and is a technique used to divine the location of underground water sources. Dowsers often use Y-shaped sticks that they hold in an upright position as they traverse the ground. When the stick points downward, the dowser then knows water is near. Expert dowsers claim to be able to measure the exact depth of underground streams, blood toxicity, cancer, oil, mineral deposits, buried treasure and many other things.

On many occasions, I've watched my grandfather water-witch using the branch of a willow tree he'd cut. Every time he did so, water was present exactly where the branch indicated.

For foretelling the future or asking questions of spirits, however, L-shaped rods are employed and held by the dowser. Dowsers often fashion these rods out of brass because it is believed the brass rods attune to the magnetic field of the earth. When held lightly, the rods move to either cross or swing open by the dowser's own sensitivity to electromagnetic energy.

You can purchase elaborately made rods from most metaphysical shops or you can make your own out of a pair of coat hangers to see if dowsing will work for you.

Dowsing Exercise

- Either purchase rods or make a pair using coat hangers and pliers to cut and bend the ends so that you have made an L-shaped pair of rods.
- Go to your inner sacred space. (See Basic Meditation Exercise.)
- Hold the rods and imagine energy coming from the Universe into you, through your hands and into the rods. Charge them with your energy.
- Ask the rods to cross.
- Ask the rods to open.
- When you get the feel of this, try asking that the rods point you in the direction of something like your car keys. (This

technique works great for finding lost items!)

- Now, invite your Guide to answer questions for you by crossing the rods for "yes" answers and opening the rods for "no" answers.

- When you are through, thank your Guide and the Universe for your gift of mediumship.

Partner Exercise with Dowsing Rods

- Ask a like-minded friend to hold the dowsing rods and sit across from you.
- Quickly find your inner sacred space.
- Mentally ask the rods to cross.
- Now, try mentally opening them.
- Try making the rods move independently of one another, all without telling your friend what you are doing.

This technique is a fun experiment with sending and receiving energy and will work best with someone whose energy and development is similar to your own.

Scrying

Scrying is a technique that involves seeing images, scenes, people or situations in a crystal ball, smoke, a bowl of water or a mirror. The word *scry* comes from the English word *descry*, which means "to make out dimly" or "to reveal".

Since the time of the ancient Greeks, diviners have used scrying techniques to see the past, present and future. Nostradamus, the famous sixteenth-century psychic, used a bowl of water as a scrying aid.

A modern-day scryer is parapsychologist Dr. Raymond Moody, who coined the term NDE or Near Death Experience. Moody founded The Dr. John Dee Memorial Theater in rural Alabama where people can go to scry in hopes of connecting with their loved ones in spirit. One of the methods Moody employs at the Theater is mirror gazing.

Mirror gazing involves staring into a mirror or other polished surface until a sort of trance state comes over the medium. Those mediums who are clairvoyant may then see hazy images in the mirror. Psychic Dr. Jeanette McClure describes her clairvoyant visions as "like watching a movie" in her mind's eye.

Many people have developed their own scrying techniques using various reflective surfaces to glean psychic information. Crystal ball, mirror or water gazing work very well for mediums whose psychic technique strength is clairvoyance. Others who are stronger in clairaudience may actually hear disembodied voices when they scry.

Scrying Exercise

- Fill a bowl to the brim with water.
- Set the bowl at the base of mirror, which is tilted so the mirror reflects a solid surface such as a blank wall.
- With very dim or no lighting, sit a few feet away from the mirror so that you cannot see your own reflection in it.
- Go to your inner sacred space. (See Basic Meditation Exercise, however, for this exercise, after you've achieved a light trance state, open your eyes.)
- Mentally call on your Gatekeeper.
- Gaze into the mirror until your vision blurs.
- Notice any impressions you receive. You may see images or faces with your physical eyes or you may only receive impressions in your mind's eye. Do you hear voices either audibly or psychically? Do you see smoke?
- When you are finished, thank those on The Other Side for communicating with you.
- Reground by eating, taking a walk outdoors or other activity.

The Ouija Board

One of the most controversial tools in the field of spirit communication is the Ouija board. In fact, many people's first experience with the paranormal is through the Ouija board. Some of these people have harrowing stories associated with Ouija board use, but the Ouija does not have to be feared. With the proper precautions and appropriate intentions, the Ouija can be a tool that advances spirit contact of all kinds.

Ouija is actually a combination of the French word, *oui*, meaning "yes", and the German word, *ja*, which also means "yes". Ouija boards are used to channel spirits who communicate by spelling out messages on a board of arranged numbers and letters. Various forms of the Ouija board have been employed throughout the centuries. As early as 600 B.C., use of the Ouija was recorded in China and also in Greece. Native Americans also created a variation of the Ouija board to find lost objects, people or to communicate with spirits of the deceased.

French Spiritualist M. Planchette, for whom the device used to indicate the letters was named, invented the concept of the modern Ouija in 1853. The first patent on the Ouija board, however, was awarded to Elijah J. Bond in 1891. In the following year, 1892, rights to the board were purchased by William Fuld and in 1966, the right to mass manufacture the board was acquired by Parker Brothers.

The Ouija has unfortunately cultivated an unfavorable reputation, even in some mediumistic circles, as a tool that attracts lower entities. Users should always remember that like attracts like in the realm of spirits and the motive behind the desire to communicate should be considered before any form of spirit contact is initiated.

The personality of the spirit being contacted should also be taken into consideration. Good information comes from entities and spirits who offer advice to help you decide what is in your best interest. Spirits who make demands or advise you to make drastic changes in your life are not higher-level entities and should be approached with caution.

The Ouija board itself is merely a focus that facilitates spirit communication and unlocks the innate intuition we all possess. The planchette is not manipulated by any mysterious unseen force. Rather, the spirits employ the energy of the user's hands. Therefore, it is relatively easy to manipulate the messages received from spirit. The user must learn to feel the answers in order to obtain accurate information.

While Using the Ouija

❖ Avoid the use of drugs and alcohol.
❖ Avoid the use of foul language and rude talk. Remember you are speaking with an entity in spirit and treat them with the same respect you would treat a person in the physical.

- ❖ Do not use the board if you are sick.
- ❖ Do not use the board if you are mentally stressed.
- ❖ Avoid subjecting yourself to movies and news that disturb you.
- ❖ Do things that will increase your own vibrations so you can better meet your spirit friends halfway. For example: Talk to other people who enjoy communicating with spirits, angels and Guides.
- ❖ Exercise and eat a healthy balanced diet.
- ❖ Spend time outdoors absorbing nature.
- ❖ Meditate. By this, I mean focus on good things in your life.
- ❖ Spend some time each day thanking the Universe for things for which you are grateful.

Ouija Exercise

How to Use the Ouija (alone or with a partner)

- Go to your inner sacred space. (See Basic Meditation Exercise.)
- Think of questions you would like to ask your Guides or meditate on a deceased

friend or family member and decide what you would like to know from them beforehand. Often, when the spirit we've been waiting to contact is finally there, we forget our questions. It may help to make a list.

- Place one or both hands on the planchette and start moving it slowly with your own energy.

- If there is a spirit present who has a message for you, you will feel the energy begin to tug and push your hand. At that point, let the spirit guide your hand. When a spirit is present, the planchette will glide effortlessly across the board. When you are manipulating the planchette, you will experience a heavy dragging sensation.

- Experiment with this phenomenon after you feel you've connected with a spirit who wants to work with you.

- You may also want to have a pen and paper handy to write down the messages you receive.

- When you are finished receiving messages from spirits, close the board with a prayer. Example: *I ask God to send the White Light through me and through this board. I thank the spirits who communicated with me and ask that God bless each one.*

Working with and being aware of energy moving through your hand takes practice. Don't get disheartened if you haven't felt anything yet. Just keep being *open to receive.*

Table Tipping

Some of my friends had attended meetings at the Parapsychology Research Institute, which was founded by Dr. Joe Slate. They suggested I give Dr. Slate a call, not only to promote a book of regional ghost stories I had written with the group but also to meet people who, like me, were interested in communicating with spirits.

At that time, I had no confidence in my mediumistic ability and had relatively little experience in communicating with disincarnate souls.

Dr. Slate invited me to a meeting, mentioning that after the program, tables would be set up so that anyone who wanted to could take part in something he called table tipping.

I'd never heard of table tipping and asked him a little about it. "Spirits come through for those present to offer knowledge and reassurance by tapping out answers with the table," he explained.

The idea that Ryan could communicate with me, one on one, through a table seemed a bit farfetched, but if it worked, I was all for trying it.

I attended the meeting with high expectations.

After a short program, Dr. Slate and others began unfolding antique bridge tables and setting them up for the table tipping. Hastily, I pulled up a chair. "Can someone explain this to me?" I asked. "I've never done it before."

"It's really quite simple," Dr. Slate said, taking the seat beside me. "The spirits use our energy to lift the table and then tap out yes and no answers in response to our questions."

Anticipation coursed through my limbs as I placed my hands on the table. I looked across the checkerboard pattern. Dr. Jeanette McClure was seated opposite me. Her name and psychic ability was known throughout north Alabama. She and Dr. Slate both had appeared on the Sci-Fi Channel's *Sightings* and Jeanette was renowned for work she had done nationwide in finding missing people and solving murder cases. Dr. Slate had written several books published by Llewellyn Worldwide. I felt lucky to be surrounded by some of the most psychically gifted people in the country.

If Ryan was indeed present, surely one of these people would pick up on the energy I was uncertain of at that time.

We placed our hands lightly on top of the table and Dr. Slate opened it with a request that we all be surrounded by white light, that only positive spirits be allowed to speak through the table and answer questions by tapping once for "yes", twice for "no" and three times for "don't know" or "maybe".

The table shifted and I closely watched everyone's hands. No one seemed to be forcibly moving the table. Ryan's presence grew strong behind me and my face and throat began to tingle. I knew this was real. This was no parlor trick. This was genuine and these people really believed that spirits were about to lift this table and speak through it.

Silently, I begged Ryan to come through for me. But would he?

The energy grew stronger and the table went up on one leg. Amazed, I watched as those participating determined with whom the spirit was there to speak. "Are you here for me?" an older lady with a long gray braid asked.

The table tapped once. *Yes.*

She and her brother asked a series of questions about a relative who had died under mysterious circumstances. I tried to pay attention but my mind was focused on Ryan. Mentally, I told him to watch what was going on. If this worked here, it might possibly work just for me alone.

The table went flat and then rose again. We determined that it was Jeanette McClure's Spirit Guide. I sat, touched, as she spoke with her Guide on a very personal level about the various things going on in her life. The Guide's presence seemed to reassure her, to give her hope. It certainly gave me hope. Hope that spirits could hear us, see us and could communicate with us. Briefly, I closed my eyes, wanting desperately for Ryan to come through and give me the same sort of reassurance Jeanette found.

Other spirits came through the table. Each energy was different. Female energy seemed soft and gentle. Male energy was a little more forceful. The energy of the Guides was remarkably strong, lifting the table and tapping out answers with a quiet but unmistakable power.

The table tipped downward into my lap.

One of the women leaned forward and looked at me. "This one is a man. I think it's for you."

I tried to swallow but my mouth had suddenly gone dry. My gaze riveted to the checked pattern on top of the worn bridge table. "Ryan?"

One tap answered me. *Yes.*

My heart soared. I had waited so long for this moment. He had heard me. The messages, the information I'd gotten from him was all real.

I took a deep breath. "Did you die in my store?"

Yes.

I squeezed my eyes shut again, trying to hold back the emotion that flooded my being. I had to test this spirit. I had to know for certain. "Did you die in 1956?"

No.

"1957?"

Yes.

He answered several other questions to my satisfaction until there was no doubt in my mind I was actually conversing with Ryan Martin.

After everyone had spoken with the spirits who'd come through for them, Dr. Slate closed the table with a prayer.

Soon after that meeting of the Parapsychology Research Institute, I bought a Samsonite table and tried, unsuccessfully, on my own to communicate with Ryan through it. The table was too heavy for him to lift with just my energy.

Undaunted, I called Jeanette McClure. She arrived and with a group of like-minded friends, we attempted to talk with Ryan through it. The energy was present, but not intense enough to raise the heavy metal Samsonite.

Just as we were about to give up, an antiques dealer I had approached earlier arrived at Martin's with a wooden-legged card table.

I unfolded the rickety legs and set it up. When I placed one hand on it, the entire table slid three feet across the tile floor.

Thus, my first tabling sessions resulted in answers being given by the table sliding one direction for yes and another for no.

A few weeks after Ryan became proficient with sliding the table, we moved it onto a carpeted surface and he lifted it onto two legs, tapping out yes and no answers for us.

My ability spread and my friends started bringing people to me who had lost loved ones. I enjoyed being able to serve as a link connecting this world to the next and providing comfort and reassurance to others. More than anything, I love being able to speak and exchange energy with the spirits around me.

Table tipping was only a beginning for me in the realm of interaction with The Other Side. It has opened me to more direct communication through telepathic means, with not only spirits but also my Guides, God, the angels and other beings that have much to teach us.

With a little patience and help from The Other Side, anyone can communicate through a lightweight card table and a group of friends who share the same interest of gaining wisdom and encouragement.

Table Tipping Exercise

- Get a lightweight card table. Spirits especially like the ones with wooden legs. Wood seems to conduct energy better than metal.

- It usually helps to have several open-minded people participate. If you know someone who has tabled before, invite them. Spirits find it easier when someone has faith it will work.

- Quickly go to your inner sacred space and encourage the other participants to relax and imagine the White Light coursing through their bodies while they are firmly grounded and connected to the Universe.

- Place your hands lightly on the table and say an opening prayer such as: *We ask God/the Creator/the Angels (any universal power in which you believe) to surround us with the White Light of protection. We invite positive spirits from the White Light to come through the table, to communicate with us by lifting the table and tapping once for "yes", twice for "no" and three times for "don't know" or "maybe" answers.*

- Wait for the spirits to come through. If they seem unable to lift the table, ask them to slide it one direction for "yes" and another for "no". Don't get discouraged. Sometimes it takes the spirits awhile to learn to work with your energy. Again, this exercise takes quite a bit of practice.

- When a spirit does come through, ask "yes" and "no" questions to determine who it is and with whom it is there to speak.

- Sometimes entities will come through the table who do not know or have messages for the participants. When this happens, request that the spirit be blessed and then ask it politely to leave.

- After a tabling session, always close the table with a prayer such as: We ask God to send the White Light through the table and around each one of us present. We ask that God bless each of the spirits who came through and thank them for coming.

Tabling can be a wonderful and life-changing experience but be careful with whom you share this. To table well, you need people with whom you are comfortable and who you trust implicitly.

Development Groups

Once you seriously begin to pursue the development of mediumistic ability, you might want to start or join a group with which to share what you are learning.

Find or create a group of like-minded people as a base of support for you. There are many such groups online. You can even start your own group on Yahoo.

I cannot stress how important it is for you to surround yourself with people who are experiencing spirit contact. Not only will these people validate your experiences, other developing mediums can boost your own ability.

Again, use step one—ask—and the manifesting techniques you have chosen to bring these people into your life.

You might want to visit a new age shop. Often these stores offer a bulletin board with group meetings or you can post your own.

If you start your own, offer a topic discussion or a speaker program. Your scope doesn't have to deal with mediumship only. Cover areas such as holistic healing, extra terrestrial contact, psychic phenomena, self-empowerment strategies and so on.

These meetings are a great way to build your ability and your confidence as a medium.

Organizing a Development Group

After you've met and clicked with other people interested in developing their ability as mediums, get a group of five to seven people together. Make a commitment to meet once a month for six months.

It is best if everyone involved can attend every meeting. The Guides learn to work with each other and with the group members. If someone quits or if someone new joins the group in mid-stream, then the Guides must assimilate the new energy that has come to the group.

To begin each meeting, everyone sits in a circle, invites their Spirit Guides to join in and all direct their energy to one member at a time. If you choose to have a speaker or topic discussion afterward, you might also practice reading for one another. Share your own success stories and concerns.

Giving Readings to Others

If you have practiced communication with spirits, receiving answers and have gotten accurate information you could validate, then you may feel you are ready to read for others.

Start by letting the Universe know that you are ready to help others with your ability.

Then be open.

We are not all going to be super mediums on TV reading for jaw-dropping crowds. But that doesn't mean you can't reach and help people in your own realm of existence.

Be open to how you will use your ability. Not all mediums are readers. Some are writers. Some may be historians or documentarians. Others may be healers, massage therapists, hypnotherapists, counselors, teachers, nurses, doctors and so on. The list is endless.

You may be a doctor who can talk to spirits. Your clients may never know you are receiving information from their Guides or concerned loved ones on The Other Side. They don't have to know for you to help them.

You may be a writer who tells your experiences and helps others develop their gift.

If you decide you want to do readings, then by all means, do so.

Talk to others you respect in the field. Check out their policies and procedures. If you are required to get a business license, do so. If you plan to charge for your services, do so. Your time is worth compensation. You wouldn't think twice about paying an attorney for legal advice. Think of yourself as a person who has worth and value and treat yourself as such. Charge accordingly. Think of it as an exchange of energies.

Always lend credibility to yourself and to what you do. Dress and act in a professional manner. Don't give readings in your living room while the television is on and your kids are racing through the house.

Be open to the beliefs and faiths of others.

Treat clients with the same confidentiality as you would expect from a doctor or counselor.

Remember, you are a channel, a medium and as such should always remain humble. You are only the vessel through which the information pours.

Are You Ready to Give Readings?

- Go to your inner sacred space. (See Basic Meditation Exercise.)
- Call on your Spirit Guide.
- Pose the question, "Is it in my best interest to use my ability to help others?" "How can I use my ability to help others?"
- Ask your Guide to present you with opportunities to help others and to use your gift.
- Be open to the answers you will receive. You might be surprised.

- Thank your Guide for providing you with insight.

If you choose to give readings for others, then you will need to develop and practice a reading style. Talk to other mediums. Attend psychic fairs. Practice giving readings with the members of your development group until you feel confident in your ability.

Giving readings can drain your energy. So can the clients for whom you read. It is important to *shield* your energy by eating well, getting enough rest and asking your Guide to surround you with protection.

Another technique developed by researcher and psychologist, Joe H. Slate, Ph.D., is the Finger Interlock Technique.

In a study funded by the U.S. Army Missile Research and Development Command, Dr. Slate discovered, through aura photography, that the aura—or energy field around every living thing—could be influenced by others. Interactions with positive people enhanced the aura and conversely contact with negative people could drain a person's energy, influencing short-term memory, health and even physical strength.

When you, as a medium, give readings to others, you are sharing their energy. It is imperative you take precautions to protect yourself.

The Finger Interlock Technique

- Bring the tips of your thumbs and middle fingers of each hand together to form two interlocking circles.
- Visualize yourself surrounded by protective White Light.
- Say aloud, "I am divinely protected and energized."

While it is fun and rewarding to give readings, you might discover you want to use your gift of mediumship for more personal reasons or to advance your own spiritual understanding. Just because you can read others does not mean you are required to do so.

Once you have asked and become open to receive then use your ability in a professional and responsible manner. At times, being able to chat with spirits is lots of fun. At other times, it's serious business.

The Law of Attraction

What do people want to know from spirits? Why bother with this at all? Are they really going to impart the secrets of the Universe?

You and the people for whom you read might be surprised!

Most people who will come to you for assistance are merely looking for validation their loved one is all right on The Other Side.

Many people who contact spirits are looking for confirmation of their beliefs. Is there a heaven? Is there a God?

Spirits will never challenge a person's faith or belief system. What you believe, you create, and therefore it is.

Many people for whom you will read want to know the answer to future questions. When will I meet my soul mate? When will I win the lottery?

When you read for others, you may find there may not be any messages about money buried in the back yard or clues as to who murdered whom. Spirits are not concerned with these issues, for the most part.

However, they are concerned with our emotional well-being and our spiritual development.

When you read for others, it is important to show them how The Other Side wants to work to fulfill their lives. In other words, show your clients how the Universe can work with them to help them find their soul mate or create wealth in their lives.

I once did a reading for Lilly, a lovely young woman who really had no expectations about the reading. She was simply curious. A female came through for her and I received the name Danielle. I picked up that Danielle was Lilly's grandmother but that Lilly had not known Danielle. In fact, Danielle was several greats removed from Lilly.

I thought it curious someone so far removed would come through for Lilly. However, Lilly was very excited. Danielle was the wife of Lilly's grandfather, a well-known Civil War general, and Lilly was in the process of raising money for the restoration of the general's home as a museum site.

The general himself came through as well and he and Danielle advised Lilly to stop focusing on the restoration and instead focus on her health and new husband. They informed her she would be getting pregnant soon and that the child would be a girl.

But Lilly had her heart set on restoring the general's home site. She proceeded with her plans, which became exhaustive and took a toll on her health. She did become pregnant and had a high-risk pregnancy. Fortunately, the child was born healthy and was named Danielle, after the grandmother.

After much heartache, Lilly decided to give up on restoring the general's home and felt she did so with her grandparents' blessing.

She told me she would have never guessed her ancestors would have been more interested in her well-being than helping Lilly to save their house but they were.

As a medium, you can enlighten your clients about their connection to The Other Side—not only to their spirit friends and Guides but to the Creator as well! Because we are a part of *All That Is*, we are also creative beings who have the ability to attract the attributes and even material things we desire to us.

I recognized Ryan's presence while I was in an abusive marriage. While I was in the midst of a nasty divorce, I asked Ryan, "When will that special someone for me come into my life?"

At that time, Ryan gave me the single most important, life-changing piece of advice anyone has ever given me. He told me, "You will never get what you want until you know what it is you want."

It was as if a light bulb flashed on over the top of my head. It was true. Up until then, I had focused on the things I didn't want in a mate. I hadn't let the Universe know what I *did* want.

There is a law in the Universe that is called the Law of Attraction.

But have you ever noticed that you often attract the thing you fear the worst? That is because you are drawing what you don't want to you without realizing it! If you live in utter terror of developing cancer, you are magnetizing the very thing you fear to you simply by focusing on it and giving it power in your life. The Universe does not understand the word "no". The Universe merely sees that you are giving thought energy to a concept. In turn, The Universe answers by providing with you with the very thing on which you expend thought energy. What you think about, you bring about.

When Ryan told me to make a list of what I wanted in a husband, I made a list of two hundred items. Then I visualized this person coming into my life.

I knew how I wanted my future husband to treat me. I wrote it all on my list. I wanted kindness, respect and, in turn, I wanted to feel that way about him.

I began to treat myself as I wanted others to treat me. I attracted good positive people who loved and respected me and nearly two years after I'd made my list, my dream man came into my life with all the attributes I requested — even as far as the eye and hair color, the kind of car he drove, the place where he lived, his interests and even his sign of the Zodiac.

I got everything I asked for.

It is important, however, to think what you want completely through.

Spirits do want us to know that we have the power to change our lives.

Attraction Exercise

- Think of something small you'd like to have or a trait you would like to possess. Think it completely through. How would having this object or trait impact your life in a positive way? Are there any negative aspects to having this object or trait? If so, you may need to rethink what you want.

- Ask the Universe to provide you with this object or trait.

- What is the essence of this object or trait you desire? For example, if you desire a diamond ring, what is the essence of having this ring? Will it bring you prestige? Will it make you feel secure? Will it bring you joy? Always whittle the essence of having an object down to an emotion. Emotions are very, very powerful.

- Affirm that you are a magnet for the good things you deserve. You are a magnet attracting your desired object or trait to yourself.

- Now imagine this object or trait in your possession. For example, if you want that diamond ring, look down at your hand and study it closely. Notice your nails, your knuckles, all the little lines, see the tiny veins and bones underneath your skin.

- Now close your eyes and see that diamond ring on your finger. Imagine how it looks on your finger. Feel the weight. See the clarity and cut of the diamond. Imagine the reaction of others when they see it on your finger. How do you feel now that you own this ring?

- Cut out a picture in a magazine of the object you desire, or a picture depicting the trait you desire, and tape it up in a place where you will see it every day. Every time you see this picture, go through the exercise of imagining having this object or trait. Do it in vivid detail.

- Be open to how this object or trait will come to you.

- Thank the Universe for providing you with this object or trait.

- Always talk about the object or trait with the sense that you are already in possession of it. If you say, "I *will get* _____" then it is always something that *will happen* in the future. If you say, "I have _____ and I am grateful to the Universe for providing me with _____" then the Universe will respond and the object will come into your life.

Higher level desires yield higher level results. If you are asking for spirituality or love or better health, you will get better results than if you are asking for a million dollars.

When you evoke the Law of Attraction, always ask for traits or objects within your realm of possession. In other words, don't ask for a million dollars if you are not already a millionaire. You cannot conceive of having a million dollars to the point of feeling the emotions involved in manifesting it. You can conceive of a hundred or a thousand dollars, however. Do it!

Manifesting takes practice. Always start with something small and build on it.

Ask your Spirit Guides for help in deciding what it is you really want.

Conclusion

In trying the exercises in this book, you've no doubt noticed some of them work better for you than others.

There are many different ways to receive psychic information. Work with each and find your niche.

Developing mediumistic ability is an ongoing pursuit that requires practice and dedication. Anyone can develop the ability to some level of proficiency. It all depends on your willingness to work with The Other Side to find your strong point in the reception of psychic information.

Whether you practice mediumship to learn to give readings or simply to enrich your own life, is totally up to you.

Delving into mediumship can be a rewarding learning experience. Wherever it takes you, I promise you a wonderful journey. Approach it with love in your heart and the Universe will respond in kind.

Suggested Reading

Beyond Reincarnation: Experiencing Your Past Lives and Lives between Lives by Joe H. Slate, Llewellyn Worldwide, Ltd., St. Paul, MN, 2005.

Metaphysical Fitness, Ten Commandments for Spiritual Being by Marilyn Campbell, Jasmine-Jade Publishing, Akron, OH, 2007.

Open Your Mind to Receive by Catherine Ponder, DeVorss and Company, Publisher, Marina del Rey, CA, 1983.

Reunions: Visionary Encounters With Departed Loved Ones by Raymond Moody with Paul Perry, Little Brown Company, New York, NY, 1994.

Scrying: The Art of Female Divination by Raymond Moody, Mockingbird Books, Covington, GA, 1996.

Secret, The by Rhonda Byrne, Atria Books/Beyond Words, New York, NY, 2006.

Index

CPSIA information can be obtained
at www.ICGtesting.com
Printed in the USA
FSHW022150030919
61693FS